BLOSSOM MAGIC

Beautiful Floral Patterns
to Color

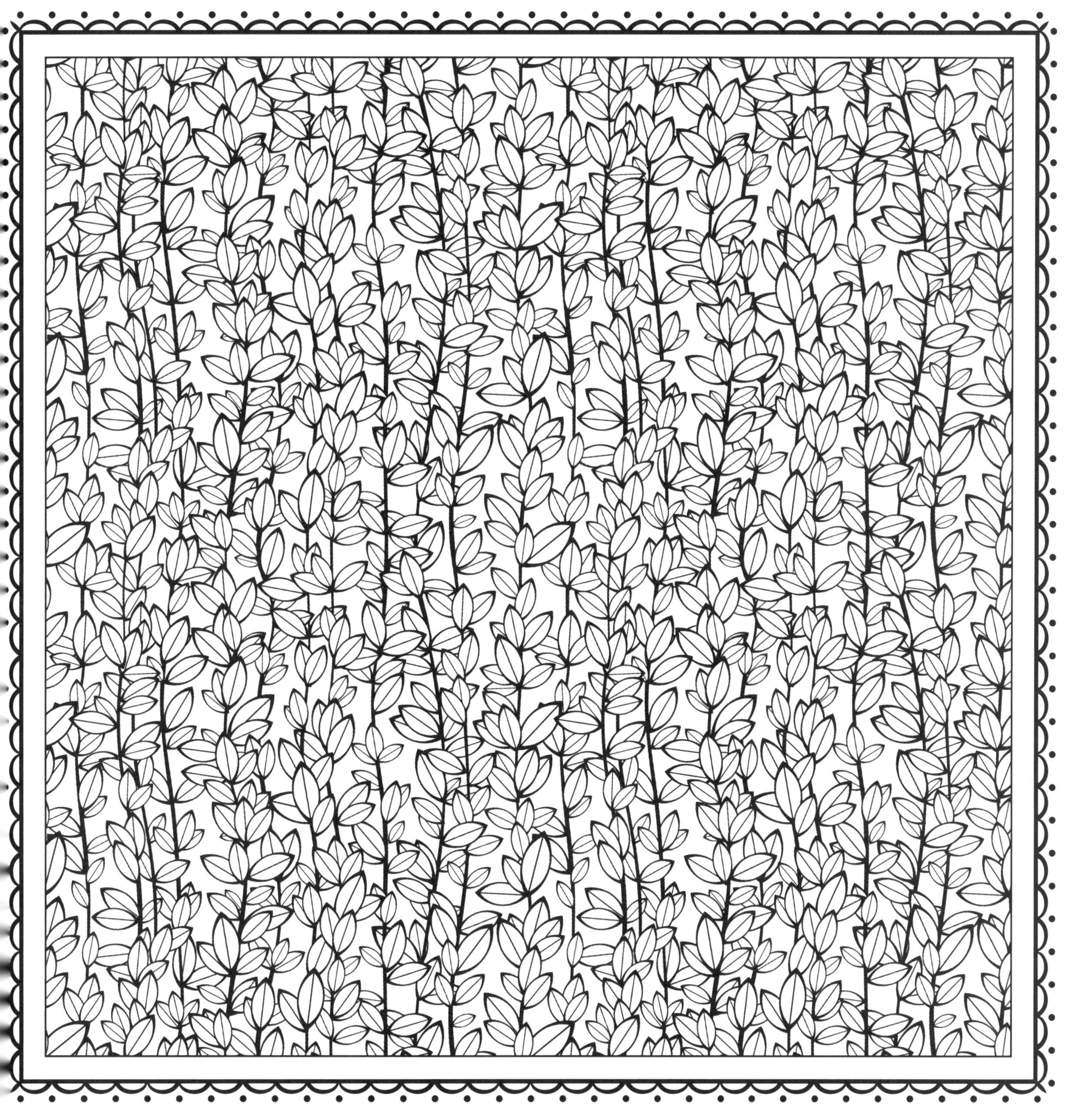

First edition for the United States, its territories
and dependencies, and Canada published in 2015
by Barron's Educational Series, Inc.

Original German title: *Blumenmeer & Gartenzauber*
© Copyright 2015 arsEdition GmbH, München

All rights reserved.
No part of this book may be reproduced or
distributed in any form or by any means without
the written permission of the copyright owner.
All inquiries should be addressed to:
Barron's Educational Series, Inc.
250 Wireless Boulevard
Hauppauge, New York 11788
www.barronseduc.com

ISBN: 978-1-4380-0731-1

Cover Design: Grafisches Atelier, arsEdition
Interior Design: Eva Schindler, Atelier für grafische Gestaltung
Illustrations: Getty Images / Thinkstock
Colorization: Laura Schindler

Printed in Canada
9 8 7 6

For best results, colored pencils are recommended.